# Lights! Camera! KIT

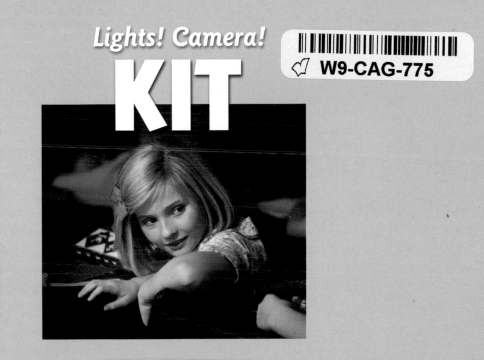

## A Behind-the-Scenes Movie Album

# MEET KIT

Kit Kittredge is a clever, determined girl growing up in the 1930s, during the hard times of the Great Depression. Kit loves to write and dreams of seeing her words in print. When her dad loses his job and her family turns its home into a boarding house in order to earn money, Kit ends up with extra chores, but also with a lot to write about—from the new boarders to the young hoboes who do chores for her family in exchange for food. But can she get published?

Kit has a nose for news—and is determined to find the culprits in a mysterious crime spree in Cincinnati.

Kit makes sure she has time to write, in spite of all her boarding-house chores.

# FROM BOOKS TO MOVIE

Kit was created as a fictional character in a series of books. Turning the Kit books into a movie script required writing and rewriting, cutting and adding, and the reshaping of certain story elements. Kit's personality and looks came from the books, as did those of most other characters. Although changes were made to Kit's story to suit the visual nature and rhythm of movie storytelling, the heart of Kit's story remains the same—what it was like to be a child growing up during the 1930s, when America was in a financial crisis. People lost their jobs and their life savings, and many even lost their homes. Life could change overnight—just as it does for the Kittredges after Dad loses his business. But as Kit learns, people also reached out to help one another through the hard times.

# THE CAST

Selecting actors for a movie is a complicated process. What makes an actor right for a role? Is it looks? Personality? Finding the right actors for all the roles in a movie is called *casting*. Talent agents suggest actors, some of whom *audition,* or perform scenes from the script while being videotaped.

Because Kit is the central character, casting that role was the most important decision for this movie. Once Abigail Breslin was cast as Kit, other performers could be selected, based in part on how they worked in relation to Abigail.

Casting agents, producers, and the director reviewed publicity photographs, or *head shots*, of hundreds of actors when deciding on the cast. Here the main casting is almost complete.

Madison Davenport is
Ruthie, Kit's best friend.

Abigail Breslin stars as Kit. Abby is
one of the youngest actors ever nominated
for an Academy Award®.

Zach Millls is Stirling,
one of the boarders.

Willow Smith is Countee,
a young hobo.

Max Theriot plays
hobo Will Shepherd.

Chris O'Donnell and Julia Ormond were cast as Kit's dad and mother.

Kit and her parents celebrate what they have to be thankful for—in spite of the hard times of the Depression.

Dad comforts Kit after telling her that he lost his business.

Kit bids her dad a tearful farewell.

Mother and Kit snap beans on the steps of their boarding house.

Stanley Tucci is Mr. Berk, one of the boarders— and a magician!

Joan Cusack plays Miss Bond, a boarder and mobile librarian.

Miss Bond doesn't believe that Mr. Berk can *levitate* her—suspend her in midair.

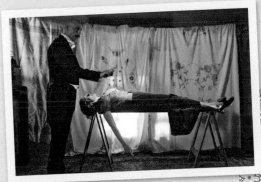

Mr. Berk asks for silence from the other boarders as he prepares to levitate Miss Bond.

Jane Krakowski was cast as Miss Dooley, a dance instructor who boards with the Kittredge family.

Wallace Shawn plays Mr. Gibson, the blustery editor of the *Cincinnati Register*.

Mr. Gibson exchanges a few words with Kit and a young reporter.

Mrs. Howard, Miss Dooley, and the kids watch Mr. Berk's magic show.

Mrs. Howard is quite nervous and very protective of her son, Stirling, whom she calls "Lamby."

Glenne Headly plays Mrs. Howard, Stirling's mother—and the first boarder at the Kittredges' boarding house.

# EXTRAS

In addition to the main cast, many actors were hired to be *extras*, or *background actors*, for the Kit movie. Like the main cast, extras wear costumes and have their hair and makeup done, but they may work for only one day or several days.

All extras, including these "protesters," get their direction from an assistant director.

Relaxing between takes

Many kids were needed as extras for Kit's movie.

Extras, such as these hobo extras, bring reality and depth to crowd scenes.

Waiting for her cue

# GOING TO THE MOVIES

Moviemaking involves hundreds of people working together to tell a story on film. As the script, director, and cast are finalized, costume and set designers, hair and makeup stylists, and other crew members start their *preproduction* work—the work done before filming actually starts.

From her beginnings as a book character and as a doll, Kit Kittredge the movie character is being brought to life!

# COSTUMES

Hundreds of costumes were made ready for the main cast and the extras. Many of Kit's costumes were based on book illustrations and doll outfits, but others were rented or created by the costume designers just for the movie.

Pages from 1930s catalogues and magazines provided costume design inspiration.

1930s dress styles featured lots of floral patterns.

Making hundreds of costumes calls for huge spools of thread!

Kit's sweater set and floral skirt were made to match the Kit doll's outfit.

A house that resembled Kit's house was rented for the six weeks of filming.

An old pickup parked on the set helps create the look of the 1930s.

## MOVIE SETS

A *set* is where filming takes place. It can be a real house, an office, or someone's backyard. Or it can be a space designed by an art director or set designer and then built as a *soundstage*. A soundstage must have extra interior space and high ceilings to accommodate film equipment.

The kitchen was one of several rooms in Kit's house that was built as a soundstage.

Kit's attic bedroom, under construction (left) and dressed for filming (right)

The set for the hobo jungle where Will and Countee stay was created along the banks of a river. Parts of the set and the set dressings almost floated away because of heavy rains just before shooting at this location!

The *Cincinnati Register* building and inside offices were actual offices dressed to reflect the style of the 1930s. Design elements such as colors, shapes, and even typefaces recall the 1930s.

Two tree houses had to be built. One was kept at the studio and used for interior scenes. The other was moved to Kit's yard and used in exterior shots.

## KIT'S TREE HOUSE

In her books, Kit dreams of having a tree house worthy of Robin Hood. In her movie, one of the most fun sets is a fantastic tree house. To make it, the set designers and builders created not only the tree house but the tree itself!

Branches were built out of wood and metal and then covered with large strips of bark created from plaster and burlap.

The tree house had to be big enough to allow access by one—and sometimes two—cameras.

After construction, the tree and the tree house were moved to the Kittredges' yard.

The inside of both tree house sets had to be dressed identically.

# SET DRESSING & PROPS

After sets are designed, set decorators and dressers use objects and interior design to make the sets look realistic. Props, short for *properties*, are items placed around a set or used by the actors in stage *business*—bits of action that make a performance more realistic.

This prop was inspired by photos of homemade scooters from the 1930s, when people made do with whatever they had—even an old orange crate.

This trunk dressed the set and also was used as a prop. Here the director explains to Abby and Madison what she wants the girls to do with it.

Dozens of old-time cars, called *picture cars*, were rented to dress scenes in which cars were used.

NEW LOW PRICE

A ladder and a bucket full of paint had to be carefully choreographed by the props master and the director for this messy scene—which was eventually cut from the movie!

Set dressing and props made the hobo jungle realistic.

The Kittredges' 1930s kitchen was brought to life by artful set dressing.

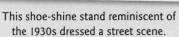

This shoe-shine stand reminiscent of the 1930s dressed a street scene.

## MONKEY BUSINESS

Whenever there are animals appearing in a movie, there are also *wranglers*, the people who work with animals. Wranglers keep the animals—and the actors who must interact with them—calm, quiet, and safe. Whether it's chickens, a dog, or a monkey, the wrangler is responsible for managing the animals and getting them to do what the script requires of them.

Abigail got to know Megs, the dog who played Grace, very well!

Dylan Smith, who plays Frederick Berk, was carefully coached by the wrangler on how to work with "Curtis" the monkey, whose real name is Ty.

The wrangler also provided and took care of the chickens that the Kittredges keep in the backyard of their boarding house.

# ACTION!

The phase when all the arrangements have been made and filming actually starts is called *production* or *principal photography*. Now everyone is ready to capture the story on film. When the cameras start rolling and the slate is clapped, the director calls out "Action!" and sets everything in motion.

Tracks laid on the street allow the camera and camera operator to move with the action on a heavy rolling *dolly*.

The slate, shown at the top of the page, is the link between the camera and the sound-recording equipment.

Even with careful planning, hundreds of decisions have to be made each day by the director and the crew.

Kit's skating is captured by two different types of moving cameras!

Like others on the set, camera operators can spend a lot of time getting ready and then have to wait to shoot. Making films is so complex and involves so many people that a lot of time is spent waiting.

Cameras placed on cranes allow for filming from a bird's-eye perspective.

The director of photography adjusts one of the lights.

# THE DIRECTOR

The director establishes the look and tone of the movie even before filming starts. When principal photography begins, she directs the actors on how to move and deliver their lines, and she consults constantly with the director of photography, the producers, the assistant directors, and other crew members to be sure that her vision of the movie is captured.

Canadian Patricia Rozema was the director of the Kit movie.

Working with an assistant director and the girls to get the right pacing for a scene

Patricia and the camera crew discuss a "dolly" shot, in which the camera moves on tracks.

Patricia and the girls in front of Kit's fabulous tree house

Patricia and director of photography David Boyd consider how best to approach a scene.

# THE PRODUCERS

The director also works closely with *producers*, the people behind the scenes who get a movie project started and see it through to completion. Executive producers are generally those in charge of finding the money to make a movie and then making many of the arrangements with a studio that will get a movie made.

Producers Terry Gould and Marissa Yeres discuss possible scene changes with Patricia.

Patricia discusses the script with producer Elaine Goldsmith-Thomas.

# HAIR & MAKEUP

An actor's day starts in the hair, make-up, and costume trailers. Hair and makeup artists keep careful records of each actor's "look" in order to match what was done in earlier scenes and to make changes for a new scene. Many touch-ups are also done throughout the day.

Abby wore a blonde wig to cover her long brown hair.

Hairstylist Cliona Fury kept Abby's wig looking good.

Jane Krakowski gets her hair and makeup refreshed at the same time.

Madison's hair had to be dyed brown to match Ruthie's hair.

The hair and makeup crews have to work fast on touch-ups between scenes.

# DOUBLES

Special actors called *doubles* replace principal actors in parts of certain scenes, such as when an actor is seen only from the back. Child actors are limited by law to about five hours of work per day, so the use of doubles allows work to continue a little longer.

Abby had to learn to roller skate, but her skating double did most of the skating.

The skating double gets her hair touched up.

Here are Abby and the Kit acting double, Alie Rutty. The Kit costumes had to be made for the doubles, too.

# SPECIAL EFFECTS

Mr. Berk's job as a magician was a bit easier than most magicians', thanks to the magic of *special effects*—film tricks done while shooting or done digitally in post-production.

But did he *really* levitate Miss Bond?

Jefferson J. Berk,
Magician Extraordinaire

Miss Bond is doubtful that Mr. Berk's magic will work.

The levitation of Miss Bond

Climbing a tree is not child's play in a movie! It involves stunt coordinators and special-effects work—and it takes a lot of time.

After Zach is secure on his branch, Madison climbs onto her branch.

Abby gets a wardrobe check before climbing the scaffolding to reach her branch.

Stunt coordinators help Abby onto her branch.

The crew had to use ladders and scaffolding, too.

The safety belts that kept the kids safe during filming will be removed digitally in *post-production*, after filming is complete.

Abby and Madison

Madison often wore a hairnet between takes to keep her curls in place.

# BEHIND THE SCENES

Between *takes*, or filmed segments, while the cameras and other equipment are being moved and made ready, the time spent waiting offers a good chance for actors to get to know one another. By law, child actors have to spend about three hours a day in school, but the rest of the time they get to hang out together.

Waiting for the slate clap and the director's call of "Action!"

Madison, Willow, and Zach look for the perfect book in Miss Bond's 1930s bookmobile.

Max and Willow try to keep warm while rehearsing a scene.

Abigail was sometimes asked for her autograph.

Abby with Erin and Brianne, newcomers who auditioned for special roles in the Kit movie

Most of the principal cast with the director and with American Girl president Ellen Brothers

The director's young daughter, Evy, and Evy's grandpa wait patiently for their scene to be called.

An extra waits to be called for her scene.

Madison and Zach *run lines*, or rehearse, between scenes.

# FUN ON THE SET

From Milaan Davenport "Ruthie"!

Thank You Cast & Crew

ERIN HILGARTNER

# IT'S A WRAP!

After months of preparation and weeks of filming, a movie *wraps* when principal photography is complete. At that point, the actors and crew go their separate ways, and the director, working with the film editor and producers, *edits* the movie, or puts it together scene by scene. Then, when the flow of the movie is just right, post-production digital enhancements are in place, and the music is added, the movie will be released—and Kit Kittredge will spring to life on the big screen!